Carousel Curriculum
Farm Animals and Farm Crops

Carousel Curriculum
Farm Animals and Farm Crops

A Literature-based thematic unit
for early learners

Bridgett Parsons, M.Ed

To order additional copies of this book, contact:
Xlibris Corporation
1-888-795-4274
www.Xlibris.com
Orders@Xlibris.com
111560

A special thanks to Helen Litterst, C.A.G.S. and Liz Cameron, C.A.G.S. for their encouragement, assistance, and friendship.

This unit is developmentally appropriate for all early learners. It is standards based and Creative Curriculum friendly. The curriculum was written by a teacher and has been used successfully with young learners including English Language Learners, children with special needs and diverse learning styles as well as homeschoolers.

INTRODUCTION

The following literature based thematic unit plan covers a 40-day period. I have used and refined these lessons over the course of 35 years of teaching early learners in both regular education settings and special education classes.

In developing these units, first I collect books on the topic. I look for a variety of fiction and non-fiction books—Big Books, books with audio tapes/CDs, books with flaps, tactile books, scratch and sniff books, books that make noises or light up, etc. I also choose different versions of the same story.

For each lesson, I select a specific unit-related concept or theme, a book/story that exemplifies this concept or theme, a related song/poem or rhyme, and a follow-up related activity (art, cooking, math, science, etc.). These concepts or themes are reflected in each lesson's "Question of the Day" and "Related Activities" sections on the Daily Lesson Plans.

Each day's lesson includes a list of materials needed for the activities, extra related activities, and several standards that are covered by the day's work.

The unit includes a list of books that can be interchanged with those on the daily plans or for extra reading times. The unit includes Center Ideas, a Poem and Song List, and extra activities listed by domain.

Additional Suggestions:

1. In the classroom, place some books in the Book Area and in other centers, but keep some specifically for Language Arts/story/circle time.
2. Choose concepts from the story that the children may not know and introduce the concepts before reading the story to help the children better understand the story.
3. Display the children's work from the units in the classroom. Save some samples of their work for evaluation purposes/recording their yearly progress.
4. Take pictures of the children with their work samples. Later in the year, these pictures can be used as a review with the children to help evaluate if they can recall information from the previous unit or tell you something about the picture.
5. When choosing related activities keep in mind that one activity can often be plugged into more than one standard and, one standard can often cover several activities.

FARM ANIMALS

OUTLINE OF WEEK 1 LESSONS

	Monday	Tuesday	Wednesday	Thursday	Friday
POEM OR SONG	Old McDonald Had a Farm	Farm Sounds	Twinkle, Twinkle, Little Star	Little Boy Blue	On A Farm
BOOK	Sally Goes To The Farm	Big Red Barn	Going To Sleep On The Farm	Rock A Bye Barn	The Farm Book
RELATED ACTIVITY	Play Tug-of-War	Graph Farm Animal Crackers	Sort basic Shapes Including "Stars"	Make an AB pattern: Cow/barn	Finger Paint Barns Red

OUTLINE OF WEEK 2 LESSONS

	Monday	Tuesday	Wednesday	Thursday	Friday
POEM OR SONG	If I Were A Farmer	Down, Down, Yellow and Brown	The Animals	This Little Cow	Take Me Out To The Barnyard
BOOK	Who Took The Farmer's Hat?	When The Leaf Blew In	The Farm Concert	Click Clack Moo	The Cow That Gets Her Wish
RELATED ACTIVITY	Go on a "Hat" Hunt	Sponge Paint Leaves	Play Rhythm Instruments	Guess How Many Milk Cartons Go In A Bag	Make A Cow Puzzle

OUTLINE OF WEEK 3 LESSONS

	Monday	Tuesday	Wednesday	Thursday	Friday
POEM OR SONG	Mary Had A Little Lamb	This Little Pig	B-I-N-G-O	Hey Diddle Diddle	If You're Happy And You Know It
BOOK	Sheep In A Jeep	Piggy In A Puddle	Dirty Harry	Ginger The Cat	Grumpy Morning
RELATED ACTIVITY	Make A Cotton Ball Sheep	Make Mud	Count Dog Biscuits	Make An Edible Cat	Make A Feeling Tree

OUTLINE OF WEEK 4 LESSONS

	Monday	Tuesday	Wednesday	Thursday	Friday
POEM OR SONG	5 Hungry Chicks	Pat A Cake	5 Little Ducks	The Turkey	Little Chicken
BOOK	Little Red Hen	Little Red Hen-Version 2	Have You Seen My Duckling	"T" For Turkey	Rosie's Walk
RELATED ACTIVITY	Sequence Story Events	Bake A Loaf Of Bread	Crack Eggs	Make Rainbow "T"s	Make Stick Puppets

DAY 1

Question of the day: What will we see on a farm?

Materials needed: a paper or wooden cubes with farm pictures glued to each side, yellow and blue watercolors, paper, paintbrushes, strips of paper, glue, rope for tug-of-war game.

Poem/Song
Old McDonald Had A Farm

Old McDonald had a farm, e-i-e-i-o.
And on that farm he had a cow, e-i-e-i-o.
With a moo-moo here and a moo-moo there,
Here a moo, there a moo, everywhere a moo-moo.
Old McDonald had a farm, e-i-e-i-o.
-continue with other verses: and on that farm he had a pig, and on that farm he had a sheep, etc.
-after each new verse, repeat the previous verses.

Book
Sally Goes To The Farm

Related Activities:

— Literacy: vocabulary development; toss a cube and name the top picture that is seen (barn, field, silo, tractor, scarecrow, etc.).

— Science: mix yellow and blue watercolors to make green, like the fields.
— Literacy: make "F" for Farm with strips of paper.
— Physical Development: play tug-of-war.

Standards Covered:

— Language: listen to and understand stories, songs, and poems.
— Literacy: learn new vocabulary.
— Science: use play to discover, question, and understand the natural and physical world.
— Literacy: know the names of some letters.
— Physical Development: participate in games that enhance physical development.

DAY 2

Question of the day: What is inside a barn?

Materials needed: large cardboard box, red paint, paintbrushes, bag, plastic farm animals, floor graph with columns for cows, horses, pigs, sheep (or those you choose), toy barn to show the children before story time.

Poem
Farm Sounds
(sung to "Wheels on the Bus")

The cow in the barn goes, "moo, moo, moo,
Moo, moo, moo, Moo, moo, moo,
(repeat)
All around the farm.
The pig in the pen goes oink, oink, oink,
The hens in the coop go cluck, cluck, cluck,
(add more farm animals).

Book
Big Red Barn

Related Activities:

— Creativity: paint a large box red to make a barn for the creative play area.

— Math: Put plastic farm animals in a bag, let a child pull out 1 animal, place animal on a floor graph (that has been pre-made with 4-5 animal columns), count how many of each animal is on the graph.
— Language: ask children what sounds various farm animals make.

Standards Covered:

— Creativity: create art projects.
— Math: match, sort, regroup, and put items in a series.
— Language: answer questions.

DAY 3

Question of the Day: What do farm animals do at night?

Materials needed: "opposites" picture cards, shape cut outs, collage materials: blue and black construction paper, glue, star stickers, cotton for clouds, chalk, moon and sun cut outs, etc., pictures of night time routines.

Poem/Song
Twinkle, Twinkle, Little Star

Twinkle, twinkle, little star,
How I wonder what you are.
Up above the world so high,
Like a diamond in the sky.
Twinkle, twinkle, little star,
How I wonder what you are.

Books
Going To Sleep On The Farm
Where Do You Sleep Little One?

Related Activities:

— Literacy: opposites card game (day/night, sleep/awake, etc.).
— Math: sort and name basic shapes including "star".

— Science: make a day collage with sun, clouds, etc. and a night collage with stars, moon, etc.
— Health: use pictures to discuss nighttime routines.

Standards Covered:

— Literacy: demonstrate understanding of "opposites".
— Math: describe and name basic shapes.
— Science: observe physical changes in their environment.
— Health: demonstrate understanding of healthy routines.

DAY 4

Question of the day: What do farm animals eat?

Materials needed: strips of paper for patterns, glue, pictures of cows and barns for patterns, picture cards of farm animals or plastic farm animals, necklace pictures for Farmer in the Dell game (farmer, wife, nurse, child, dog, cat, rat, cheese), pictures of foods that farm animals eat.

Poem
Little Boy Blue

Little Boy Blue come blow your horn.
The sheep is in the meadow.
The cow is in the corn.
Where is the little boy, that looks after the sheep?
He's in the haystack, fast asleep!

Book
Rock-A-Bye Barn

Related Activities:

— Math, AB pattern: cow/barn/cow/barn/etc.
— Language: memory game using farm animal picture cards.
— Movement: play the game, Farmer In The Dell.
— Science: match pictures of farm animals to the foods they eat.

Standards Covered:

— Math: children show an interest in recognizing and creating patterns.
— Language: think and talk about play experiences.
— Music/Movement: participate in musical activities.
— Science: make observations on real life experiences.

DAY 5

Question of the day: What do farm animals give to us?

Materials needed: barns cut from heavy duty paper, red finger paint, pictures of farm animals for cutting out, scissors, glue, pictures of or plastic farm animals, pictures or toy foods that we get from farm animals, laminated names and pictures of farm animals, ABC letters to use to spell farm animal names and to find their initials.

Poem
On A Farm
(sung to "London Bridge Is Falling Down")

Animals live on a farm, on a farm, on a farm,
Animals live on a farm, with a farmer.
Cows and pigs live on a farm, on a farm, on a farm.
Cows and pigs live on a farm, with a farmer.
-Goats and sheep live on a farm,
-Hens and chicks live on a farm,
-Dogs and cats live on a farm.

Book
The Farm Book

Related Activities:

— Creativity: each child finger paints an oak tag barn.
— Science: children cut out pictures of farm animals and glue them onto finger painted barns.
— Literacy: children match "initials" to farm animal names.
— Science: place plastic farm animals with plastic foods they give us.

Standards Covered:

— Creativity: enjoy participating in a variety of art experiences.
— Science: demonstrate knowledge of a farm environment.
— Literacy: be able to recognize and name some letters of the alphabet.

DAY 6

Question of the day: What jobs does a farmer have?

Materials needed: small straw hats (found in craft stores), paper dolls, clothes for dolls cut from denim and cloth, crayons or markers, photos of each child's face, toy tools or pictures of tools used by a farmer.

Poem
If I Were A Farmer
(sung to "Did You Ever See A Lassie?")

Oh, if I were a farmer, a farmer, a farmer,
Oh, if I were a farmer, what would I do?
I would milk the cows each morning,
Each morning, each morning,
I would milk the cows each morning, that's what I'd do. continue and use:
I would gather eggs for breakfast,
I would sow seeds in the garden,
I would feed the hens and chickens, etc.

Book
Who Took The Farmer's Hat?

Related Activities:

— Language: hide small straw hats around the room, the children search and find the hats, the children tell "where" they found their hats. (under the table, on the chair, behind the book, etc.)
— Creativity: the children draw faces on paper dolls, dress the dolls with denim pants, fabric shirts, and photos of themselves for the faces.
— Social Studies: make a chart of tools/supplies a farmer uses.

Standards Covered:

— Language: talk about play experiences.
— Creativity: create art projects.
— Social Studies: demonstrate knowledge of a farmer's work and the tools he needs and uses.

DAY 7

Question of the day: What movements can farm animals make?

Materials needed: cut out leaves, paints, sponges, straws, objects for children to try to move by blowing straws, leaves (real, paper, plastic), songs or CDS to listen to while moving like farm animals.

Poem
Down, Down, Yellow and Brown

Down, down, yellow and brown,
Leaves are falling,
Down, down.

Book
When The Leaf Blew In

Related Activities

— Creativity: use sponges to paint cut out leaves.
— Science: give each child a straw, let them blow through straws to try to move objects. (feathers, leaves, blocks, confetti, cars, etc.)
— Math: children collect and bring in leaves—count how many yellow leaves and how many brown leaves they have—talk about more/less. If no real leaves are available use paper or craft leaves.
— Physical Development: move like farm animals—run, jump, kick, etc.

Standards Covered:

— Creativity: work with various media to create art.
— Science: make observations through play.
— Math: demonstrate knowledge of 1-1 correspondence while counting, and the concept of more/less.
— Physical Development: demonstrate strength and stamina in movement activities.

DAY 8

Question of the day: What do farm animals say?

Materials needed: plastic/or pictures of farm moms and babies, rhythm band instruments, paper, crayons or markers, CDS of classical music.

Poem
The Animals
(sung to "Skip To My Lou")

Who are the animals that live on the farm,
Who are the animals that live on the farm,
Who are the animals that live on the farm,
Let us learn their names.

A duck is an animal that lives on the farm.
A duck is an animal that lives on the farm.
A duck is an animal that lives on the farm.
Now we learned her name.
(continue with other animal names)

Book
The Farm Concert

Related Activities:

— Science: using plastic animals or picture cards, match baby animals with their moms and introduce their names (cow-calf).
— Music: introduce instruments and have a rhythm band concert.
— Creativity: draw pictures while listening to music.

Standards Covered:

— Science: vocabulary for names of baby farm animals.
— Music: introduce instruments, participate in musical activities using a variety of materials for expression and representation.

DAY 9

Question of the Day: What is a cow?

Materials Needed: cow made with rubber glove udder, milk, same size empty milk cartons, various size grocery bags, chocolate milk mix, paper cups, chart paper, marker.

Poem
This Little Cow

This little cow eats grass.
This little cow eats hay.
This little cow drinks water.
And this little cow does nothing.
This cow lies and sleeps all day.
(hold up and open hand, after each line bend one finger until all fingers are folded and sleeping)

Book
Click, Clack, Moo

Related Activities:

— Science: milk a cow; prepare a cow cutout using heavy paper, add a rubber glove for the udder, prick a tiny hole at fingertips, add milk to glove, let children milk the cow.

— Math: guess how many milk cartons will fit into various size bags.
— Math: make chocolate milk, graph which milk is more popular—white or chocolate.

Standards Covered:

— Science: ask questions based upon discoveries made while playing.
— Math: begin to predict.
— Math: begin to graph.

DAY 10

Question of the day: What are the body parts of a cow?

Materials needed: cow puzzle, cow puzzles for the children to work, felt for spots, scissors, glue, numbered cows, bag of felt spots,

Poem
Take Me Out To The Barnyard
(sung to "Take Me Out To The Ball Game")

Take me out to the barnyard,
Take me out right now.
Show me the cows, pigs, and horses, too.
I hear an oink and a neigh and a moo.
There are chickens laying their eggs.
If they don't lay it is a shame.
Oh, it's one, two, three eggs today,
And I'm glad I came.

Book
The Cow That Gets Her Wish

Related Activities:

— Creativity: complete a cow puzzle, add udder, horns, tail, spots.

— Math: have cows with numbers on them, children put on corresponding number of spots on the cow.
— Literacy: children use letters/letter stickers to spell "COW".

Standards Covered:

— Creativity: demonstrate care and persistence when involved in art projects.
— Math: demonstrate knowledge of number and numeral relationships.
— Literacy: identify some letters in print.

DAY 11

Question of the day: What is a sheep?

Materials needed: paper plates, cotton balls, glue, small pieces of construction paper (for eyes, nose, etc.), rhyming picture cards, laminated sheep with interchangeable faces of various colors.

Poem/Song
Mary Had A Little Lamb

Mary had a little lamb, little lamb, little lamb.
Mary had a little lamb, it's fleece was white as snow.
And everywhere that Mary went, Mary went, Mary went,
Everywhere that Mary went, the lamb was sure to go.

Book
Sheep In A Jeep

Related Activities:

— Literacy: play a matching game with rhyming picture cards.
— Creativity: make a sheep with paper plates, glue cotton balls on for fleece.
— Math: colors: say poem "Baa, Baa, Black Sheep". Repeat the rhyme saying a different color. A child picks up the correct color head and puts it on the sheep.

Standards Covered:

— Literacy: recognize and generate rhymes.
— Creativity: use various art media to create projects.
— Math: recognize and name basic colors.

DAY 12

Question of the day: What is a pig?

Materials needed: brown paint, shaving lotion, plastic pigs, bin to mix the mud, cut out paper pigs, brown finger paint, chocolate pudding mix, farm animal crackers, picture cards of "opposites", "P" cut out, pictures or stamps of "P" words such as pig, puddle, pink.

Poem
This Little Pig Went To The Market

This little pig went to the market.
This little pig stayed home.
This little pig ate roast beef.
This little pig had none.
This little pig cried, weee-weeeee, all the way home.
—while saying the poem pull a finger on a hand or a toe on a foot, continue until the little pig cried and tickle the child.

Book
Piggy In A Puddle

Related Activities:

— Science: make mud (brown paint and shaving lotion) for plastic pigs to roll in.

— Creativity: put fingerprint dirty spots onto cut out pigs.
— Science: make chocolate pudding, add pig animal crackers, eat.
— Literacy—opposites: dry/wet, dirty/clean.
— Literacy: "P" for Pig, Puddle, Pink.

Standards Covered:

— Science: investigate changes in materials.
— Creativity: use various tools to create art projects.
— Literacy: demonstrate knowledge of "opposites" and recognize some letters of the alphabet in print.

DAY 13

Question of the day: What is your dog's name? (What name would you choose for a dog?)

Materials needed: ABC cards, name cards for each child, various sizes of real dog biscuits, dog bowl, chart story written by the teacher about a dog (with blanks throughout, the teacher will ask a child what word he wants to put in the blank), marker.

Poem/Song
BINGO

There was a farmer had a dog and BINGO was his name-o.
B-I-N-G-O, B-I-N-G-O, B-I-N-G-O,
And BINGO was his name-O!
-repeat but clap for B (do not say B)
-repeat for each letter until you clap 5 times.

Book
Dirty Harry

Related Activities:

— Literacy: use letters and spell BINGO. Look at their name cards and answer questions about them, ex. How many letters are in your name, what letter does your name start with, do you have 2 of the same letter in your name?

— Math: sort real dog biscuits by size.
— Math: ask child to give you a specific number of dog biscuits, he/she counts and puts that number into a dog bowl.
— Language: The teacher presents an outline of a simple story about a dog. The children can fill in the blanks to create an original chart story. (for example: My dog is _____. His name is _____.)

Standards Covered:

— Literacy: children know the letters in their names.
— Math: compare objects according to size.
— Math: use 1-1 correspondence in counting objects.
— Language: participate in a discussion about a topic.

DAY 14

Question of the day: What do cats like to do?

Materials needed: Oreos, M&M's, licorice, napkins, laminated and numbered cats, fish crackers, pictures of people handling kittens and cats, pictures of cats eating, climbing, cleaning, etc.

Poem
Hey Diddle, Diddle

Hey diddle, diddle, the cat and the fiddle.
The cow jumped over the moon.
The little dog laughed to see such a sport,
And the dish ran away with the spoon.

Book
Ginger The Cat

Related Activities:

— Creativity: make an edible black cat, use Oreos for the face, M&M's for the eyes, licorice for the whiskers.
— Math: have laminated cats with numbers on them, the children count out fish crackers and put the correct amount on the cats.
— Health: discuss the proper way of handling kittens and cats.

Standards Covered:

— Creativity: use various media to make art projects.
— Math: use 1-1 correspondence to count objects.
— Health: learn proper and safe ways to handle pets and take care of them.

DAY 15

Question of the day: What makes you grumpy?

Materials needed: a large laminated tree with Velcro pieces on it, several copies of faces showing the emotions: happy, sad, sick, scared, excited, grumpy, etc. with Velcro on the back, journals, pencils.

Poem/Song
If You're Happy And You Know It

If you're happy and you know it clap your hands.
If you're happy and you know it clap your hands.
If you're happy and you know,
Then your face should surely show it.
If you're happy and you know it clap your hands.
Repeat with: stomp your feet, shout Hooray, etc.

Book
Grumpy Morning

Related Activities:

— Language: talk about our feelings. Make a feeling tree where children can post a face showing how they feel each morning.
— Physical Development: play "Follow The Leader".

— Literacy/Writing: write in journal (those that can not write can draw a picture and dictate words for the teacher to write). They can write about a farm animal or how they are feeling.

Standards Covered:

— Language: communicate needs or thoughts through actions, expressions and words.
— Physical Development: demonstrate body and space awareness to move and stop with control over speed and direction.
— Literacy: begin to dictate ideas, sentences, and stories. Understand that writing carries a message.

DAY 16

Question of the day: What is a hen?

Materials needed: paper plates, crayons, red feathers, glue, items for eyes and beaks, pictures of story events to sequence, plastic or pictures of hens and chicks.

Poem
5 Hungry Chicks

Said the first little chicken with a queer little squirm,
"I wish I could find a fat little worm."
Said the second little chicken with an odd little shrug,
"I wish I could find a fat little bug."
Said the third little chicken with a sharp little squeal,
"I wish I could find some yellow corn meal."
Said the fourth little chicken with a sigh of grief,
"I wish I could find a little green leaf."
Said the fifth little chicken with a faint little moan,
"I wish I could find a wee gravel stone."
"Now see here said the mother from the green garden patch,
If you want any breakfast, just come here and scratch."

Book
Little Red Hen

Related Activities:

— Creativity: make a paper plate hen, glue red feathers onto body.
— Literacy: sequence 3 of the story events.
— Math: count out 5 chicks for a mom hen.
— Math: put the chicks in a line, let the children point out which one is first, second, third, fourth, fifth. Put the children in a line and have them say who is fifth, second, first, fourth, third.

Standards Covered:

— Literacy: be able to sequence story events.
— Math: work with ordinal numbers.
— Creativity: children express an interest in art activities.

DAY 17

Question of the day: How do you make bread?

Materials needed: bread mix; bowl; mixing spoon; slices of wheat, white and cinnamon bread; graph paper, marker, play-doh, "B" stamps.

Poem
Pat-A-Cake

Pat-a-cake, Pat-a-cake, Baker's man.
Bake me a cake as fast as you can.
Roll it, pat it, mark it with a B.
Put it in the oven for baby and me.

Book
Little Red Hen (different version)

Related Activities:

— Science: bake a loaf of bread.
— Science: taste wheat bread, white bread, cinnamon bread and graph favorite.
— Creativity/Literacy: use play-dough or clay and make "cakes", stamp them with "B's".

Standards Covered:

— Science: make simple observations.
— Health: begin to understand that some foods have nutritional value.
— Literacy: demonstrate awareness of beginning sounds of words.

DAY 18

Question of the day: What farm animals have feathers?

Materials needed: plastic feathered farm animals (or pictures of), possible someone to bring in incubator and eggs and set up in room, real eggs to crack and observe, tray, bowls, spoons, glue, paints, cut out paper eggs.

Poem
5 Little Ducks

Five little ducks went out to play
Over the hills and far away.
When the mother duck went, "quack, quack, quack",
4 little ducks came waddling back.
-continue the count down until 0 ducks came waddling back.
No little ducks went out to play
Over the hills and far away,
When the father duck went, "quack, quack, quack"
Five little ducks came waddling back.

Books
Have You Seen My Duckling
The Chick And The Duck

Related Activities:

— Science: sort farm animals that have feathers from those that do not.
— Science: have incubator in room to watch eggs hatch.
— Science: crack eggs and observe shell and what is inside.
— Creativity: wash and dry cracked egg shells, use this as mosaic, glue pieces onto cut out egg, paint if you want, or leave white.

Standards Covered:

— Science: make observations and predictions.
— Science: explore the natural processes of development.
— Creativity: appreciate and demonstrate respect for the work of others.

DAY 19

Question of the day: What is a turkey?

Materials needed: papers with black "T"s on them, crayons or markers, drawing paper, paint, feathers.

Poem
The Turkey

The turkey is a funny bird.
His head goes wobble, wobble.
The only word that he can say is
Is gobble, gobble, gobble.

Book
"T" For Turkey

Related Activities:

— Literacy: make a rainbow "T" for turkey.
— Creativity: make fingerprint turkeys. Take a small amount of paint and brush it on your hand and press down on the paper. Let dry, use markers to draw eyes, legs, beak and glue small feathers on the body.

Standards Covered:

— Literacy: know the names of some letters of the alphabet and hear the beginning sounds of words.
— Creativity: demonstrate persistence in making art projects.

DAY 20

Question of the day: How do feathered farm animals move?

Materials needed: a map of Rosie's route, pictures of places on her route, glue, craft sticks, cut outs of Rosie and the fox, crayons, cut out eggs or egg stickers, straw, construction paper.

Poem
Little Chicken

I had a yellow chicken by the old barn gate.
And that little chicken was my playmate.
That little chicken went cluck, cluck, cluck.
Then he ran away, to play with a little duck.

Book
Rosie's Walk

Related Activities:

— Literacy: sequence the route that Rosie walked.
— Literacy: make stick puppets of Rosie and the Fox.
— Language: children retell the story using stick puppets.
— Creativity: make a nest of straw, glue cut out eggs, or egg stickers in the nest.

Standards Covered:

— Literacy: sequence story events.
— Literacy: discuss characters in the book.
— Language: children retell a story or parts of a story using props.
— Creativity: children express their ideas through art projects.

FARM BOOKS

A

A COW ON THE LINE
A FRIEND FOR FLASH
A PIG IS BIG
A PILE OF PIGS
A PLUMP AND PERKY TURKEY
A VISIT TO THE FARM
ACROSS THE STREAM
ALL PIGS ARE BEAUTIFUL

B

BABY ANIMAL FRIENDS
BABY FARM ANIMALS
BARK GEORGE
BARNYARD TRACKS
BIG RED BARN
BISCUIT GOES TO SCHOOL

C

CHICKEN LITTLE
CITY PIG
CLICK CLACK MOO
CLIFFORD'S FAMILY
COCK-A-DOODLE MOO
COLOR FARM
COWS CAN'T FLY

D

DAISY AND THE EGG
DIRTY HARRY
DOWN BY THE POND
DRIVE A TRACTOR
DUCK ON A BIKE

E

F

FARM
FARM ALPHABET BOOK
FARM COUNTING BOOK
FARM ANIMALS
FARM MORNING
FARMER
FARMER DUCK
FARMING
FARM-TOUCH AND FEEL
FRIEND FOR FLASH

G

GINGER THE CAT
GOING TO SLEEP ON THE FARM
GOOD NIGHT FARM
GRUMPY MORNING

H

HAVE YOU SEEN MY DUCKLING
HELLO LITTLE PIGLET
HENNY PENNY
HERD OF COWS! FLOCK OF SHEEP!
HOW TO BE A CAT

I

I WENT WALKING
I WENT TO A FARM AND WHAT DID I SEE
INSIDE A BARN IN THE COUNTRY
IN THE RAIN WITH BABY DUCK

J

K

L

LITTLE PINK PIG
LITTLE RED HEN
LITTLE WHITE DUCK

M

MAISY'S MORNING ON THE FARM
MILK
MILLIONS OF CATS
MINERVA LOUISE
MR. BROWN CAN MOO, CAN YOU?
MRS. WISHY-WASHY
MRS. WISHY-WASHY'S FARM
MY BARN
MY FIRST FARM
MY FIRST FARM FRIENDS

N

O

OLD MCDONALD HAD A FARM
ON THE FARM
ON GRANDPA'S FARM
ONE HORSE WAITING FOR ME
OPEN THE BARN DOOR

P

PEEK A MOO
PERFECT THE PIG
PIG SURPRISE
PIG, PIG GETS A JOB
PIGS FROM 1-10
PIGGY IN A PUDDLE
PIGGIES
PIGS,PIGS,PIGS,PIGS
PIGS IN A BARROW

Q

R

ROCK-A-BYE FARM
ROSIE'S WALK
RUN, TURKEY, RUN

S

SALLY GOES TO THE FARM
SHEEP IN A JEEP
SLEEPY DOG
SNAPPY LITTLE FARMYARD
SOUNDS ON THE FARM
SUDDENLY
SPOTS, FEATHERS, AND CURLY TAILS

T

'T' FOR TURKEY
TEN FAT TURKEYS
THE CHICK AND THE DUCK
THE COW THAT GETS HER WISH
THE COW THAT WENT OINK
THE FARM BOOK
THE FARMER
THE FARM CONCERT
THE LITTLE DUCK
THE MILK MAKERS
THE PATCHWORK FARMER
THE PIGGY IN THE PUDDLE
THE RUSTY, TRUSTY, TRACTOR
THE SCARECROW
THE SCARECROW'S DANCE
THE SCARECROW'S HAT
THE THREE BILLY GOATS GRUFF
THE THREE LITTLE DUCKS
THE THREE LITTLE KITTENS
THE THREE LITTLE PIGS
THE THREE LITTLE WOLVES AND THE BIG BAD PIG
THE YEAR AT MAPLE HILL FARM
TIME FOR BED
TO MARKET, TO MARKET
TOP CAT
TRACTOR
TURKEYS

U

V

W

WE KEEP A PIG IN THE PARLOR
WHEN THE LEAF BLEW IN
WHERE DO YOU SLEEP LITTLE ONE?
WHO TOOK THE FARMER'S HAT?
WHO SAYS QUACK?

X

Y

YOU'RE A WINNER, TRACTOR MAC

Z

FARM POEMS AND SONGS

Old McDonald Had A Farm

Old McDonald had a farm, e-i-e-i-o.
And on that farm he had a cow, e-i-e-i-o.
With a moo-moo here and a moo-moo there,
Here a moo, there a moo, everywhere a moo-moo.
Old McDonald had a farm, e-i-e-i-o.
-continue with, and on that farm he had a pig, and on that farm he had a
sheep, etc.
-after each new verse, repeat the previous verses.

Farm Sounds
(sung to "Wheels on the Bus")

The cow in the barn goes, "moo, moo, moo,
Moo, moo, moo, Moo, moo, moo,
(repeat)
All around the farm.
The pig in the pen goes oink, oink, oink,
The hens in the coop go cluck, cluck, cluck,
(add more farm animals).

Little Boy Blue

Little Boy Blue come blow your horn.
The sheep is in the meadow.
The cow is in the corn.
Where is the little boy, that looks after the sheep?
He's in the haystack, fast asleep!

Twinkle, Twinkle, Little Star

Twinkle, twinkle, little star,
How I wonder what you are.
Up above the world so high,
Like a diamond in the sky.
Twinkle, twinkle, little star,
How I wonder what you are.

On A Farm
(sung to "London Bridge Is Falling Down")

Animals live on a farm, on a farm, on a farm,
Animals live on a farm, with a farmer.
Cows and pigs live on a farm, on a farm, on a farm.
Cows and pigs live on a farm, with a farmer.
-Goats and sheep live on a farm,
-Hens and chicks live on a farm,
-Dogs and cats live on a farm.

If I Were A Farmer

(sung to "Did You Ever See A Lassie?")
Oh, if I were a farmer, a farmer, a farmer,
Oh, if I were a farmer, what would I do?
I would milk the cows each morning,
Each morning, each morning,
I would milk the cows each morning, that's what I'd do. continue and use:
I would gather eggs for breakfast,
I would sow seeds in the garden.

Down, Down, Yellow and Brown

Down, down, yellow and brown,
Leaves are falling,
Down, down.

The Animals
(sung to "Skip To My Lou")

Who are the animals that live on the farm,
Who are the animals that live on the farm,
Who are the animals that live on the farm,
Let us learn their names.

A duck is an animal that lives on the farm.
A duck is an animal that lives on the farm.
A duck is an animal that lives on the farm.
Now we learned her name.
(continue with other animal names)

This Little Cow

This little cow eats grass.
This little cow eats hay.
This little cow drinks water.
And this little cow does nothing.
This cow lies and sleeps all day.
(hold up and open hand, after each line bend one finger until all fingers are folded and sleeping)

Take Me Out To The Barnyard
(sung to "Take Me Out To The Ball Game")

Take me out to the barnyard,
Take me out right now.
Show me the cows, pigs, and horses, too.
I hear an oink and a neigh and a moo.
There are chickens laying their eggs.
If they don't lay it is a shame.
Oh, it's one, two, three eggs today,
And I'm glad I came.

Mary Had A Little Lamb

Mary had a little lamb, little lamb, little lamb.
Mary had a little lamb, it's fleece was white as snow.
And everywhere that Mary went, Mary went, Mary went,
Everywhere that Mary went, the lamb was sure to go.

This Little Pig Went To The Market

This little pig went to the market.
This little pig stayed home.
This little pig ate roast beef.
This little pig had none.
This little pig cried, weee-weeeee, all the way home.
—while saying the poem pull a finger on a hand or a toe on a foot, continue until the little pig cried and tickle the child.

BINGO

There was a farmer had a dog and BINGO was his name-o.
B-I-N-G-O, B-I-N-G-O, B-I-N-G-O,
And BINGO was his name-O!
-repeat but clap for B (do not say B)
-repeat for each letter until you clap 5 times.

Hey Diddle, Diddle

Hey diddle, diddle, the cat and the fiddle.
The cow jumped over the moon.
The little dog laughed to see such a sport,
And the dish ran away with the spoon.

If You're Happy And You Know It

If you're happy and you know it clap your hands.
If you're happy and you know it clap your hands.
If you're happy and you know,
Then your face should surely show it.
If you're happy and you know it clap your hands.
Repeat with: stomp your feet, shout Hooray, etc.

5 Hungry Chicks

Said the first little chicken with a queer little squirm,
"I wish I could find a fat little worm."
Said the second little chicken with an odd little shrug,
"I wish I could find a fat little bug."
Said the third little chicken with a sharp little squeal,
"I wish I could find some yellow corn meal."
Said the fourth little chicken with a sigh of grief,
"I wish I could find a little green leaf."
Said the fifth little chicken with a faint little moan,
"I wish I could find a wee gravel stone."
"Now see here said the mother from the green garden patch,
If you want any breakfast, just come here and scratch."

Pat-A-Cake

Pat-a-cake, Pat-a-cake, Baker's man.
Bake me a cake as fast as you can.
Roll it, pat it, mark it with a B.
Put it in the oven for baby and me.

The Turkey

The turkey is a funny bird.
His head goes wobble, wobble.
The only word that he can say is
Is gobble, gobble, gobble.

Little Chicken

I had a yellow chicken by the old barn gate.
And that little chicken was my playmate.
That little chicken went cluck, cluck, cluck.
Then he ran away, to play with a little duck.

5 Little Ducks

Five little ducks went out to play
Over the hills and far away.
When the mother duck went, "quack, quack, quack",
4 little ducks came waddling back.
-continue the count down until 0 ducks came waddling back.
No little ducks went out to play
Over the hills and far away,
When the father duck went, "quack, quack, quack"
Five little ducks came waddling back.

Five and Five Eggs

Five and five eggs, that makes ten. (hold up hands)
Sitting on top is mother hen. (fold one hand over the other)
Crackle, crackle, crackle, (clap three times)
What do I see? (put fingers around eyes)
Ten fluffy chickens as yellow as can be. (hold up 10 fingers)

P-I-G-G-Y
(sung to BINGO)

There was a hungry little hog,
And Piggy was his name-o.
P-I-G-G-Y, P-I-G-G-Y, P-I-G-G-Y,
And Piggy was his name-o.

I'm a Little Piggy

I'm a little piggy, short and stout.
Here are my ears and here is my snout.
When I see the Farmer in the dell,
I oink, oink, oink, and wiggle my tail.

Five Farmers

Five little farmers woke up with the sun.
It was morning and the chores must get done.
The first little farmer went out to milk the cow.
The second little farmer thought he'd better plow.
The third little farmer found and pulled the weeds.
The fourth little farmer planted more seeds.
The fifth little farmer drove his tractor round.
Five little farmers, the best that could be found.

The Pig in Mud

The little pig rolled in the mud.
Squishy, squashy, it felt so good.
The farmer pulled the piggy out.
Oink, oink, oink, the pig did shout.

To Market, To Market

To market, to market,
To buy a fat pig,
Home again, home again,
Jiggidy, jig.

Baa, Baa, Black Sheep

Baa, baa, black sheep.
Have you any wool,
Yes sir, yes sir,
Three bags full.

Farmer In The Dell

The farmer in the dell,
The farmer in the dell,
Hi-Ho the Derry-o, the farmer in the dell.
The farmer takes a wife, the farmer takes a wife,
Hi-Ho the Derry-o, the farmer takes a wife.
-continue with:
The wife takes a child,
The child takes a dog,
The dog takes a cat
The cat takes a rat,
The rat takes the cheese.
The cheese stands alone. Hi-Ho the Derry-o, the cheese stands alone.

Bobby Joe the Scarecrow

Bobby Joe is filled with hay,
Down on the farm.
Oh, will he scare the crows away?
Way down on the farm.
Oh, the crows are here
And they want to stay.
Bobby Joe, Bobby Joe,
Can you make them fly away?
Bobby scared the crows away.
Way down on the farm.

Black Cat Caper

5 black cats were sitting on the fence.
The first one said, "The moon is so immense."
The second one said, "There are ghosts floating by."
The third one said," I heard an owl's cry."
The fourth one said, "Let's hide right away."
The fifth one said, "I wish it was day."
"Whooooooooooo," went the wind, and out went the light.
And the five black cats scampered out of sight.

I Went To The Farm

I went to the farm!
I met some new friends,
A cow in the barn,
And a pig in the pen.
I went to the farm!
My buddies were there-
The sheep and the goats,
And a gentle old mare.

The Animals Go In And Out

The animals go in and out, in and out,
In and out, in and out.
The animals go in and out of the barn.

This Little Pig

This little pig likes to play through the night
And through the day.
With an oink, oink, oink, he's on his merry way.
Rolling in the mud and eating hay.

Listen To The Animals

Listen to the animals, What do they say?
The cow says, "Moo,"
And the horse says, "Neigh."
The sheep says, "Baa",
And the hen says, "Cluck."
Now who says "Quack"?
Why, it's the duck!

Milk The Cow

Milk, milk, milk the cow.
Milk her every day.
Give her water, salt, and grass,
And lots of yellow hay!

FARM ANIMALS UNIT—CENTER IDEAS

DRAMATIC PLAY AREA (Add the following to this play area.)

- Big Barn—made from large cardboard box
- Stuffed farm animals
- Farm animal costumes
- Farmer's clothes
- Stool
- Milking pail
- Farmer's tools
- Real horse saddle
- Toy horse to sit on/ stick horses
- Toy tractor
- Scarecrow
- Large picture of a barn to tape on the wall in this center
- Real bale of hay, if no one is allergic
- Decorate with real pumpkins and corn stalks.

BLOCK AREA (Add the following to this play area.)

- Toy barn
- Toy farm animals
- Tractor, other farm vehicles
- Toy farmer and family
- Cover boxes with brown paper (hay bales) to stack.

DISCOVERY AREA

- Put plastic ducks in the water table.
- Put tractors and farm animals in the sand table.
- Add to the Sand table small tools such as hoes, rakes, shovels.
- Bring an incubator and eggs to the classroom.
- Have grass and dirt to examine, use magnifying glasses.
- Make Mud (real) or brown paint mixed with shaving lotion.
- Examine wool from a sheep.
- Sort seeds.
- Plant seeds and observe growing plants.
- Bake bread.
- Play with bottles filled with oil, water, food coloring. Shake bottles, observe.
- Put real straw (or raffia) in the empty water table, hide plastic farm animals or plastic eggs in the straw.

LIBRARY AREA (Add the following to this area.)

- Books on farm animals
- Books on farms
- Books on farmers
- Books on barns and farm buildings
- Books on CD or tapes

TOYS AND GAMES AREA (Add the following to this area.)

- Puzzles of farm animals
- Memory game, using farm pictures
- Lacing farm animals
- Store bought games that have a farm theme.

ART AREA

- Paint a large cardboard box to make a barn for dramatic play area.
- Paint cut out barns. Staple 2 together, cut out a door to see inside.
- Color and cut out animals to glue inside the above barn.
- Make a paper doll farmer, denim pants, children's photos for face.
- Make farm animals-stick or paper bag puppets.
- Make farm animals-use various media such as yarn, cotton ball, wool, felt, feathers, paper plates, toilet paper rolls.
- Create a farm scene—use crayons, stickers, foam shapes.
- Use paints, tempera, watercolors, finger paints.
- Manipulate Play-dough.
- Stamps with farm item stamps.
- Wash and dry eggshells to make mosaics.
- Paint with feathers.
- Paint with sponges.
- Create "Red" collages.
- Make a horse tail: roll up newspaper, tape one end, fringe the other end into long strips.

MUSIC AND MOVEMENT AREA

- Old McDonald Had A Farm
- The Farmer In The Dell
- Play Country and Square Dancing music.

ADDITIONAL FARM ACTIVITIES LISTED BY DOMAIN

MATH ACTIVITIES

- Make AB patterns (ABC patterns) using farm animals and farm items: cow/barn or cow/barn/pig.
- Count plastic farm animals, count how many legs they have.
- Use 1-1 correspondence to count fish crackers to match the number on numbered laminated cats.
- Graph our favorite farm animal.
- Use measuring tools to bake a loaf of bread.
- Graph our favorite bread.
- Make farm animals, barn, or tractor using shapes.
- Introduce the colors red (for barn) and green (for grass).
- Sort farm animals by one characteristic.
- Use number stamps.
- Use number cookie cutters and play dough.
- Name basic shapes including "star".
- Make farm animals, barn, tractor using shapes.
- Count eggs/introduce the word "dozen".
- Write numbers using a quill.
- Introduce names of coins, name or count coins as you drop them into a piggy bank.

LITERACY/WRITING ACTIVITIES

- Write in a farm journal—have stickers of farm animals; for those not able to write, a teacher can print and the child can trace or copy.
- Write with a feather.
- Write with chalk, pencils, markers.
- Write with fingers in sand/salt.
- Use sticker letters to spell words from unit.
- Have laminated unit related word cards/children can trace with dry—erase markers.
- Play with felt or sand sticker letters/tactile letters.
- Make play dough letters.
- Learn sign language alphabet—this is a good fine motor lesson.
- Use wooden pieces to make letters.
- Mazes—children help the farmer get back to his barn.
- Trace written letters.
- Decorate large cut out letters with stickers of items starting with that letter; stamp the same letter around the larger decorated letter.
- Use letter stamps to spell a child's name.
- Search for letters in magazines and papers, highlight them.
- Cut out letters to use in spelling words.
- Play with ABC stamps.
- Play with picture cards that show opposites, story sequencing and rhyming words.
- Use puppets to retell stories, or parts of stories.
- Use felt board characters from stories, children can retell stories or make up new stories using these characters.
- Play with "store bought" characters. (such as "Babe" the pig)
- Play "rhyming" game-such as the name game: example (Mary, Mary, Bo Bary, Banana, Fana, Fo, Fary, Fee, Fi, Mo, Mary, MARY).
- Have pictures of events that happened in a story and events that did not happen. Let the children sort them.

SCIENCE ACTIVITIES

- Sort animals with feathers from other animals.
- Crack and investigate eggs.
- Have plastic eggs that open and plastic animals; children put the animals that hatch inside the eggs and place the others in a box.
- Introduce toy or real farm tools and teach children how these tools are used by the farmer.
- Put grass, roots, and dirt in a box for children to investigate. (add magnifying glasses, colored lens, etc.)
- Make piglet snacks-spread strawberry jam onto a rice cake, use sliced strawberries for ears, use raisins for eyes, use banana slices for noses.
- Match farm animals to their silhouettes.

ART ACTIVITIES

- Make collages using red items and green items.
- Make farm animals-use children's handprints for bodies, add features with markers, crayons, or paint.
- Make paper doll farmers.
- Make stick puppets.
- Paint large and small barns.
- Make a farm mural.
- Make scarecrows—stuff real clothing, add paper bag head, straw, etc.
- Make paper costumes of farm animals.
- Make turkey placemats-use wax paper or clear contact paper.
- Make headbands—use stretch ribbon, add animal ear cut outs.
- Fingerpaint with chocolate pudding (mud).
- Cut fringes on green construction paper to make fields of farm grass.
- Lace farm animals.
- Make mud (mix brown paint and shaving lotion) and paint with it.
- Sponge paint leaves.
- Draw a glass shape on white construction paper, draw a picture or letter on each glass, children paint the glass with watercolors, like magic, the picture or letter appears.
- Dip colored chalk in buttermilk and draw pictures.

PHYSICAL DEVELOPMENT ACTIVITIES

- Play *Tug-Of-War.*
- Play *Follow The Leader.*
- Play *Duck, Duck, Goose. (game rules are below)*
- Make an obstacle course. Go over, under, through, around, across, etc.
- Play *Farmer In The Dell. (game rules are below)*
- Play *Pin The Tail On The Donkey.*
- Play *Farmer, May I? (game rules are below)*
- Move like farm animals: walk, run, hop, jump, waddle, climb, trot, etc.
- Children use flippers (swimming flippers) to walk like a duck.
- Role play goats-provide soft balls for the children to butt with their heads like goats.
- Play horseshoes.
- Parachute play—place stuffed farm animals in the center of the parachute and make them hop and jump.
- Use balloons for animals, try to keep them from landing on the floor.

GAME RULES

DUCK, DUCK, GOOSE

Children sit in a circle.
One child is chosen to be the TAPPER.
This child walks around the circle gently tapping each child's head as she passes them. She also says either "DUCK" or "GOOSE".
If she says "DUCK", the tapped child sits and the TAPPER continues to walk. If the TAPPER says "GOOSE", she runs and the tapped child tries to catch her. The TAPPER runs around the circle and sits in the spot vacated by the child chasing her. If she is caught, she goes into the middle of the circle. Now the other child becomes the TAPPER.

THE FARMER IN THE DELL

The children form a circle. They hold hands and slowly walk in a circle while singing the "Farmer In The Dell" song.
The teacher has picture card necklaces of the characters in the song.
She gives the farmer necklace to a child that moves into the center of the circle. The children continue walking and singing around the farmer. The farmer "picks" a wife, he gives the picture to a friend, who joins him inside the circle. The wife picks a child, so forth . . . .
When the cheese stands alone, the other characters reenter the circle, so the cheese is all alone.

FARMER, MAY I?

The children stand in one long line, a teacher or a child is the caller.
The caller stands at the other end of the room facing the line.
The caller gives directions such as," Mary, take two baby steps."
Mary must ask, "Farmer, may I?" The caller says, "Yes, you may."
If the child forgets to ask the farmer's permission they must stay in line, if they have moved previously, they must return to their starting place.
The first child to reach the caller is the winner, and becomes the caller.

FARM CROPS

OUTLINE OF WEEK 1 LESSONS

	MONDAY	TUESDAY	WEDNESDAY	THURSDAY	FRIDAY
POEMS/ SONGS	Farm Chores	Chores	Tractor Song	The Floppy Scarecrow	Colorful Crows
BOOKS	Who Took The Farmer's Hat?	Farmer Duck	You're A Winner Tractor Mac	The Scarecrow's Dance	The Scarecrows Hat
RELATED ACTIVITY	Go On A Hat Hunt	Play Memory Game	Use Shapes To Make A Tractor	Make Cornmeal Play-dough	Make A Scarecrow Puzzle

OUTLINE OF WEEK 2 LESSONS

	MONDAY	TUESDAY	WEDNESDAY	THURSDAY	FRIDAY
POEM/ SOND	Mr. Carrot	Dig A Little Hole	One Potato, Two Potato	Cornstalk	Pick Up The Squash
BOOK	The Carrot Seed	The Turnip	The Biggest Potato	Raccoons In Ripe Corn	Stone Soup
RELATED ACTIVITY	Root A Carrot	Taste A Real Turnip	Mash Potatoes	Husk Corn	Make Vegetable Soup

OUTLINE OF WEEK 3 LESSONS

	MONDAY	TUESDAY	WEDNESDAY	THURSDAY	FRIDAY
POEM/ SONG	Way Up High In The Apple Tree	Red Apple	Apples Here	Apples	Apples
BOOK	Apple Trouble	Big Red Apple	10 Apples Upon Top	Apple Pie Tree	Apple Farmer Annie
RELATED ACTIVITY	Lace Paper Apples	Sequence Apples By Size	Count 1-10 Apples	Bake An Apple Pie	Estimate # Of Apples In A Basket

OUTLINE OF WEEK 4 LESSONS

	MONDAY	TUESDAY	WEDNESDAY	THURSDAY	FRIDAY
POEM/ SONG	The Pumpkins Are Here	I'm A Little Pumpkin	1 Little, 2 Little Pumpkins	JACKO	Pumpkin
BOOK	16 Runaway Pumpkins	Biggest Pumpkin Ever	Spookley, The Square Pumpkin	Bumpy Little Pumpkin	From Seed To Pumpkin
RELATED ACTIVITY	Paint Pumpkins Orange	Play With Orange Play-Dough	Weigh Pumpkins	Sort Bumpy/ Smooth Items	Make A Pumpkin Seed Mosaic

DAY 1

Question of the day: What chores does a farmer have?

Materials needed: paper doll farmers cut out, denim pants cut out, little straw hats, photos of children's faces, picture cards of a farmer's tools

Poem
Farm Chores

Five little farmers woke up with the sun.
It was early morning and the chores must be done.
The first little farmer went out to milk the cow.
The second little farmer thought he'd better plow.
The third little farmer cultivated weeds.
The fourth little farmer planted more seeds.
The fifth little farmer drove his tractor round.
Five little farmers, the best that can be found.

Book
Who Took The Farmer's Hat?

Related Activities

— Creativity: make farmer paper dolls, with denim pants, straw hat, photos of children for the faces.
— Math: put the farmer paper dolls in a line and label; first, second, etc.

— Language: go on a "straw hat" hunt; children answer the question, "Who found the hat?"
— Science: use picture cards and talk about the tools a farmer needs to do his chores.

Standards Covered

— Creativity: explore various roles in dramatic play through the use of props and language.
— Math: use counting and number vocabulary as part of play.
— Science: collect information through pictures.

DAY 2

Question of the day: Can you name some fruits and vegetables that a farmer grows?

Materials needed: various fruits and vegetables, knife to cut food, small paper plates and napkins, farm picture cards, plastic fruits and vegetables, picture cards of fruits and vegetables

Poem
Farm Chores

This is the way we pull the weeds, pull the weeds,
Pull the weeds.
This is the way we pull the weeds,
So early in the morning.
(make up verses: drive the tractor, mow the hay, etc.)

Book
Farmer Duck

Related Activities

— Science: uses senses to investigate various vegetables and fruits (touch, smell, taste, look at shapes and colors).
— Language: play memory game with farm pictures.

— Math: sort vegetables and fruits by color/shapes (use real, plastic, or pictures of fruits and vegetables).

Standards Covered

— Science: use their senses to make observations, gather and record information.
— Language: develop conversation during daily activities and games.
— Math: sort objects according to one characteristic.

DAY 3

Question of the day: What is a tractor?

Materials needed: cut out shapes for making a tractor, glue, sheets of brown paper to glue the tractor on, paints, gardening tools, white painting paper, toy tractors and plows

Poem
Tractor Song

The wheels on the tractor go round and round,
Round and round, round and round.
The wheels on the tractor go round and round,
All around the farm.
(add verses: tractor goes back and forth, farmer goes up and down, etc.)

Book
You're A Winner, Tractor Mac

Related Activities

— Math: make a tractor using shapes.
— Creativity: paint with gardening tools. (trowel, small rake, etc.)
— Science: play with dirt/potting soil; make tracks, rows, with toy tractors and plows.

— Physical Development: play Wheelbarrow Game.(a child holds a partner's feet as they walk with their hands like a wheelbarrow)

Standards Covered

— Math: describe and name common shapes.
— Creativity: experiment with different tools to create projects.
— Science: use play to discover, question, and understand the natural and physical world.
— Physical Development: initiate activities that challenge their bodies in new ways.

DAY 4

Question of the day: What does a scarecrow do?

Materials needed: real clothing for use in making a scarecrow, paper for stuffing the scarecrow, paper bag for head, facial features cut out or markers, hat, bandana, play-dough, cornmeal, black crows cut out and laminated, CDs of country and square dance music

Poem
The Floppy Scarecrow

The floppy, floppy scarecrow,
Guards his fields all day.
He waves his floppy, floppy hands,
To scare the crows away!

Book
The Scarecrow's Dance

Related Activities

— Creativity: make a real scarecrow with stuffed clothes, paper bag head, straw hat, bandana.
— Science: make cornmeal play-dough.
— Math: count crows, give the children a number and they count out that many crows.

— Music/Movement: dance to country western and square dance music.

Standards Covered

— Creativity: demonstrate care and persistence when involved in art projects.
— Science: investigate changes in materials and cause-effect relationships.
— Math: begin to associate a number of objects with names and symbols for numbers.
— Music/Movement: use movement and a variety of musical styles to express feelings.

DAY 5

Question of the day: What color is a crow? What does a crow eat?

Materials needed: scarecrow puzzle for each child (cut apart), paper on which to glue the puzzle pieces, glue, cut out white crows, black paint, straw for painting, seeds, chart paper, markers

Poem
Colorful Crows

Scarecrow (child's name),
Standing all alone.
Shoo that (color) crow back to its home.
(have laminated crows of various colors on the floor, when it is a child's turn he get the crow of the color names and shoos it away)

Book
The Scarecrow's Hat

Related Activities

— Math: make a scarecrow puzzle.
— Creativity: paint cut out crows black; paint with straw.
— Literacy: play a rhyming game. (think of words that rhyme with colors: blue/shoe, etc.)
— Science: sort seeds.

Standards Covered

— Math: children show an interest in creating puzzles.
— Creativity: experiment with different tools to create.
— Literacy: recognize and generate rhymes.
— Science: use their senses to make observations.

DAY 6

Question of the day: What is a carrot?

Materials needed: carrots, plastic cups, water, toothpicks, items to measure with, rulers, cut out carrots, "C" stamps, inkpad or paint

Poem
Mr. Carrot

Nice Mr. Carrot makes curly hair.
His head grows under the ground.
His feet are in the air.
Early in the morning I find him in his bed.
I give his feet a great big pull, and out comes his head!

Book
The Carrot Seed

Related Activities

— Science: root a carrot. (Place a carrot root end down in a jar and cover 1/3 of the root with water, use toothpicks to keep the top out of the water.)
— Math: measure lengths of carrots.
— Literacy: "C" for carrot—glue or stamp "C"s on a cut out carrot.

Standards Covered

— Science: explore the natural processes of growing.
— Math: explore measurement.
— Literacy: know the names of some letters.

DAY 7

Question of the day: What is a turnip?

Materials needed: raw turnip, cooked turnip, paper bags, paper for stuffing bag, purple paint, paint brushes, green paper for leaves, pictures of the characters in the story

Poem
Dig A Little Hole

Dig a little hole, plant a little seed.
Pour a little water, pull a little weed.
Give a little sunshine, grow a little bean.
It grows big, and gets green and greener.

Book
The Turnip

Related Activities

— Science: taste a raw and a cooked turnip.
— Creativity: make a paper bag turnip. (Stuff a lunch bag, paint purple, add leaves.)
— Literacy: sequence story events. (Sequence order of characters as they appear in the story.)

Standards Covered

— Science: use their senses to make observations.
— Creativity: enjoy participating in a variety of art experiences.
— Literacy: be able to sequence events from a story.

DAY 8

Question of the day: What is a potato?

Materials needed: boiled potatoes, potato mashers, small plates, spoons, napkins, potatoes for stamping, paint, white painting paper, potatoes for counting

Poem
One Potato, Two Potato

One potato, two potato,
Three potato, four,
Five potato, six potato,
Seven potato, More!

Book
The Biggest Potato

Related Activities

— Physical Development: boil potatoes, let the children use potato mashers to make mashed potatoes.
— Creativity: use potato halves to stamp/print designs.
— Math: count potatoes, make sets and say which has more/less potatoes.

Standards Covered

— Physical Development: demonstrate increasing strength and stamina to perform fine motor skills.
— Creativity: demonstrate care and persistence when involved in art projects.
— Math: use words such as more than and less than to express number concepts.

DAY 9

Question of the day: What is a cornstalk?

Materials needed: corn for husking (one per child), popcorn to pop, picture cards of vegetables, paint, paper for painting, real cornstalk, ruler

Poem
Cornstalk

I'm a cornstalk tall and straight,
Tall and straight, tall and straight.
I'm a cornstalk tall and straight,
And my corn tastes just great!

Book
Raccoons In Ripe Corn

Related Activities

— Physical Development: each child gets an ear of corn, have a corn husking race (cook and eat the corn).
— Science: make popcorn.
— Literacy: use picture cards and talk about vegetables (shape, color, names) play a memory game with the picture cards.
— Creativity: let the cobs dry, use them to put in paint and roll designs onto paper.

— Math: measure height of a real cornstalk (use standard and nonstandard forms of measurement).

Standards Covered

— Physical Development: discriminate between a variety of smells, textures, and tastes.
— Literacy: develop vocabulary.
— Creativity: plan and create paintings and prints.
— Math: measure height using standard and nonstandard forms of measurement.

DAY 10

Question of the day: Do you like vegetable soup?

Materials needed: big pot, ladle, water, stone, vegetables cut up, spices, cut out paper bowls, ABC cereal or pasta, glue, pictures of healthy and unhealthy foods

Poem
Pick Up The Squash

Pick up the squash and put it in the basket,
Pick up the squash and put it in the basket,
Pick up the squash and put it in the basket,
Pick up all the squash!
(continue naming different vegetables: have these vegetables spread on the floor and let children gather them as they are named)

Book
Stone Soup

Related Activities

— Science: make "Stone Soup"—(first add a washed stone to the pot as in the book) have an assortment of vegetables on hand, ask a child to add a specific vegetable to the pot, continue until all vegetables are ready to cook, add spices, make soup.

— Literacy: cut out paper bowls (one for each child), the child glues ABC cereal or pasta onto the bowl (the child can name the letters in his/her soup).
— Physical Development: children name or sort pictures of healthy food from unhealthy food.

Standards Covered

— Science: explore temperature and cause-effect relationships based on experiences.
— Literacy: children will know the letters in their own names.
— Physical Development: begin to understand that some foods have nutritional value.

DAY 11

Question of the day: Where do apples grow?

Materials needed: large red apples cut out, green yarn or lacing string, real apples, knife for slicing, pan, sugar, cinnamon, recipe written on chart paper for making applesauce, measuring cups and spoons, small cups and spoons for each child

Poem
Way Up High In The Apple Tree

Way up high in the apple tree,
Two little apples smiled at me.
I shook that tree as hard as I could.
Down came the apples,
Mmmmmm, they were good!

Book
Apple Trouble

Related Activities

— Physical Development: lace apples.
— Math: cut an apple to see the star.
— Science: make applesauce.

Standards Covered

— Physical Development: use hand-eye coordination to perform fine motor tasks.
— Math: describe shapes found in the natural environment.
— Science: make observations based on real life experiences.

DAY 12

Question of the day: What shape is an apple?

Materials needed: paper apples for children to cut out and color, scissors, crayons, "A" stamps or stickers, ink pad or paint, paper apples of different sizes for each child, strip of paper on which to glue the sequenced apples, glue

Poem
Red Apple

A little red apple hanging on a tree.
The juiciest apple you ever did see.
The wind came past and gave an angry frown.
And that little apple cam tumbling down.

Book
Big Red Apple

Related Activities

— Literacy: stamp "A"s onto cut out apples.
— Math: sequence apples by size.
— Physical Development: play game, *"Upset the Fruit Basket"* (directions in Physical Development Activities page).

Standards Covered

— Literacy: demonstrate growing awareness of the beginning sounds of words.
— Math: sequence items by size.
— Physical Development: demonstrate body and space awareness to move and stop with control and balance.

DAY 13

Question of the day: What color are apples?

Materials needed: 1-10 apple cut outs or stickers, glue, photos of each child, paper to glue their photos and apples; sliced red, green, and yellow apples; chart paper for graph, markers

Poem
Apples Here

Apples here, apples there,
Apples are everywhere.
Some are red, some are yellow.
Please give one to this hungry fellow.

Book
10 Apples Upon Top

Related Activities

— Math: count 1-10 apples.
— Math: taste red, yellow, and green apples. (graph your favorite)
— Creativity: have children's photos, let them put 10 apple stickers stacked upon their heads.

Standards Covered

— Math: use 1-1 correspondence in counting objects.
— Math: begin to recognize and name the basic colors.
— Creativity: appreciate and demonstrate respect for the work of others.

DAY 14

Question of the day: What can we make with apples?

Materials needed: brown and green paper, glue, scissors, red circle stickers, green tissue paper, apple pictures cut apart (one for each child) for a puzzle, paper on which to glue the apple puzzle, glue, all the ingredients for making an apple pie (pan, crust, roller, apples, sugar, cinnamon, butter)

Poem
Apples

Pick some apples off the tree,
Off the tree, off the tree.
Pick some apples off the tree,
Some for you and some for me.

Book
Apple Pie Tree

Related Activities

— Science: bake an apple pie.
— Creativity: make a tissue paper apple tree, put red circle stickers on the tree for apples.
— Math: make an apple puzzle.

Standards Covered

— Science: use their senses to predict what may happen.
— Creativity: children express an interest in art.
— Math: children demonstrate a knowledge of basic shapes.

DAY 15

Question of the day: Are apples a healthy food?

Materials needed: apples (real or plastic), baskets of varying sizes. Felt board with tree and apple felt pieces

Poem
Apples

Red and juicy, shiny, sweet,
Apples you're so good to eat.
Crisp and crunchy, healthy, too,
This core is all that's left of you!

Book
Apple Farmer Annie

Related Activities

— Math: estimate the number of apples that will fit into various sized baskets.
— Literacy: have the children place apples on the tree, behind the tree, beside the tree, etc. (use felt apples and apple tree for felt board).

Standards Covered

— Math: demonstrate ability to make estimates.
— Literacy: demonstrate an understanding of locations; on, under, beside, next to, etc.

DAY 16

Question of the day: What is a pumpkin?

Materials needed: pictures of a pumpkin field for each child, crayons, pumpkin stickers, plastic pumpkins, paper plates, orange paints and brushes, string for lacing, hole punch

Poem
The Pumpkins Are Here

The pumpkins are here, the pumpkins are there.
The pumpkins, the pumpkins are everywhere.
The pumpkins are up, the pumpkins are down.
The pumpkins, the pumpkins are all around.
The pumpkins are in, the pumpkins are out.
The pumpkins, the pumpkins are all about.
The pumpkins are low, the pumpkins are high.
The pumpkins, the pumpkins all say, "Good-bye!"

Book
16 Runaway Pumpkins

Related Activities

— Math: each child has a picture of a pumpkin field, they draw or glue on 16 pumpkins.

— Literacy: using small plastic pumpkins, give the children directions to follow on where to put them (up, down, in, out, high, low, etc.).
— Creativity: paint two paper plates orange, lace them together to make a pumpkin.

Standards Covered

— Math: use 1-1 correspondence in counting objects.
— Literacy: demonstrate understanding of opposites; up/down, in/out; high/low, etc.
— Creativity: use various medium to create projects.

DAY 17

Question of the day: What is inside a pumpkin?

Materials needed: several different sizes of pumpkins, measuring tape, knife, spoon, paper towels, large "P" cut out for coloring or decorating, orange play-dough, decorating items (glitter, stickers, beads, etc.), glue, crayons

Poem
I'm A Little Pumpkin

I'm a little pumpkin, orange and round.
Here is my stem, there is the ground.
When I get all cut up, don't you shout.
Just open me up, and scoop me out.

Book
Biggest Pumpkin Ever

Related Activities

— Math: measure the "circumferences" of different size pumpkins.
— Science: cut open a real pumpkin, scoop out the seeds.
— Literacy: large "P" (P for pumpkin) cut outs for decorating; write or trace the "P" letter and decorate; make orange play-dough "P"s.

Standards Covered

— Math: perform measuring "circumferences" of objects.
— Science: use senses to gather information.
— Literacy: show an interest in the beginning sounds of words.

DAY 18

Question of the day: What shape is a pumpkin?

Materials needed: different shapes of foam or felt, black paper for facial features, glue, scissors, scales, pumpkins and gourds (real or plastic)

Poem
1 Little, 2 Little, 3 Little Pumpkins

1 little, 2 little, 3 little pumpkins,
4 little, 5 little, 6 little pumpkins,
7 little, 8 little, 9 little pumpkins,
10 little pumpkins here!!

Book
Spookley, The Square Pumpkin

Related Activities

— Math: use different shapes to create unique jack-o-lanterns.
— Science: use scales to weigh pumpkins and gourds.
— Language: participate in discussions about the pumpkins they created in the math activity.

Standards Covered

— Math: show an interest in shapes and patterns.
— Science: use scientific tools to gather information.
— Language: participate in discussions around a topic.

DAY 19

Question of the day: How do we use pumpkins?

Materials needed: smooth and bumpy items, foam ABC letters, glue, strips of paper to make name cards, ingredients needed for making a pumpkin pie (pan, crust, mix, spices, whipped cream), recipe printed on chart paper for making a pumpkin pie

Poem/Song
J-A-C-K-O

There was a pumpkin with a face, and
JACKO was his name-O.
J-A-C-K-O, J-A-C-K-O, J-A-C-K-O,
And JACKO was his name-O!

Book
Bumpy Little Pumpkin

Related Activities

— Science: sort bumpy/smooth items.
— Literacy: spell their names (use letters cut from magazines or foam sticker letters).
— Math: use measuring cups/spoons to make a pumpkin pie.

Standards Covered

— Science: demonstrate knowledge of bumpy/smooth objects.
— Literacy: recognize their name in print.
— Math: learn how to use measuring tools in cooking.

DAY 20

Question of the day: How does a pumpkin grow?

Materials needed: sequencing pictures for the growth of a pumpkin, paint a pumpkin on large paper, orange paint and brushes, pumpkin seeds, glue

Poem
Pumpkin

One day I found two pumpkin seeds.
I planted one and pulled the weeds.
It sprouted roots and a big, long vine.
A pumpkin grew and I called it mine.
The pumpkin was round and fat.
I really am proud of that.
But there is something I will admit,
That has me worried quite a bit.
I ate the other seed, you see.
Now will it grow inside of me?

Book
From Seed To Pumpkin

Related Activities

— Literacy: sequence the growth of a pumpkin (story events).

— Creativity: paint a pumpkin and glue on pumpkin seeds for a mosaic.
— Math: use pumpkin seeds to discuss more/less and few/lot.

Standards Covered

— Literacy: be able to sequence story events.
— Creativity: take pride in one's work.
— Math: use vocabulary more/less and few/lot in making comparisons of amounts.

FARM CROPS UNIT

BOOK LIST

A VISIT TO THE FARM
APPLES AND PUMPKINS
APPLE FARMER ANNIE
APPLE PIE TREE
APPLE TROUBLE
BIGGEST PUMPKIN EVER
BIG RED APPLE
BUMPY LITTLE PUMPKIN
DO THE DOORS OPEN BY MAGIC?
DORA'S EGGS
DRIVE A TRACTOR
FARM
FARM ALPHABET BOOK
FARM COUNTING BOOK
FARM COUNTRY AHEAD
FARMER
FARMER DALE'S RED PICKUP TRUCK
FARMER DUCK
FARMING
FROM PEANUTS TO PEANUT BUTTER
FROM SEED TO PUMPKIN
GREGORY, THE TERRIBLE EATER
HOW DO APPLES GROW?

I SHOP WITH MY DADDY
I WENT TO A FARM AND WHAT DID I SEE
IF YOU GIVE A PIG A PANCAKE
IT LOOKED LIKE SPILT MILK
JACK AND THE BEANSTALK
JAMIE O'ROURKE AND THE RUN AWAY POTATO
JOHNNY APPLESEED
LET'S VISIT AN APPLE ORCHARD
LITTLE RED HEN
LUNCH
MAISY'S MORNING ON THE FARM
MOUSE MESS
MRS. MCNOSH AND THE GREAT BIG SQUASH
ON THE FARM
PUMPKIN, PUMPKIN
RACCOONS AND RIPE CORN
SOMETHING GOOD
SPOOKLEY, THE SQUARE PUMPKIN
STONE SOUP
TEN APPLES UPON TOP
THE CARROT SEED
THE ENORMOUS WATERMELON
THE FARMER
THE LEGEND OF SPOOKLEY, THE SQUARE PUMPKIN
THE MARVELOUS MARKET
THE NEW BLUE TRACTOR
THE RELATIVES CAME
THE RUSTY, TRUSTY TRACTOR
THE SCARECROW
THE SCARECROW'S DANCE
THE SCARECROW'S HAT
THE TINY SEED
THE TURNIP
THE YEAR AT MAPLE HILL FARM
THERE GOES A FARM TRUCK
TODAY IS MONDAY
TO MARKET, TO MARKET
TOPS AND BOTTOMS
TRACTOR

TREMENDOUS TRACTORS
THE VERY HUNGRY CATERPILLAR
WHO STOLE THE COOKIES?
WHO TOOK THE FARMER'S HAT?
YOU'RE A WINNER, TRACTOR MAC
16 RUNAWAY PUMPKINS

FARM CROPS UNIT

POEMS/SONGS

SUN IS COMING UP

Sun is coming up,
Farmer's out the door,
He will go to milk the cows,
And start his daily chores.
Sun is going down,
Horse is in the stable,
All the fields are planted now,
Supper's on the table.

MAKING BUTTER BOOGIE

Shake it up, shake it down,
Shake it, shake it all around.
Shake it high, shake it low,
Shake it, shake it, to and fro.
Shake it over, shake it under,
Pretty soon, you'll have butter.

THE FLOPPY SCARECROW

The floppy, floppy scarecrow,
Guards his fields all day.
He waves his floppy, floppy, hands,
To scare the crows away!

PUMPKIN

One day I found two pumpkin seeds.
I planted one and pulled the weeds.
It sprouted roots and a big, long vine.
A pumpkin grew and I called it mine.
The pumpkin was round and fat.
I really am proud of that.
But there is something I will admit,
That has me worried quite a bit.
I ate the other seed, you see.
Now will it grow inside of me?

I'M A LITTLE SCARECROW

I'm a little scarecrow stuffed with hay.
Here I stand in a field all day.
When I see the crows,
I like to shout, "Hey! You crows, you better get out!"

APPLE SEED

Once a little apple seed
Was planted in the ground.
Down came the raindrops
Falling all around.
Out came the bright sun
As bright as bright can be,
And the little apple seed
Grew up to be an apple tree!

THE PUMPKINS ARE HERE

The pumpkins are here, the pumpkins are there.
The pumpkins, the pumpkins are everywhere.
The pumpkins are up, the pumpkins are down.
The pumpkins, the pumpkins are all around.
The pumpkins are in, the pumpkins are out.
The pumpkins, the pumpkins are all about.
The pumpkins are low, the pumpkins are high.
The pumpkins, the pumpkins all say, "Good-bye!"

FARM CHORES

Five little farmers woke up with the sun.
It was early morning and the chores must be done.
The first little farmer went out to milk the cow.
The second little farmer thought he'd better plow.
The third little farmer cultivated weeds.
The fourth little farmer planted more seeds.
The fifth little farmer drove his tractor round.
Five little farmers, the best that can be found.

TRACTORS, TRACTORS

Tractors, tractors, tractors help farmers work.
They pull plows that break up the clumps of dirt.
The farmer can work much faster
Because he has a tractor.
There's lots to do the whole year through.
Tractors help farmers do the work.

SHOVELS, RAKES, AND EVEN HOES

Shovels, rakes, and even hoes,
Help the farmer as he sows.
First, he digs into the ground;
Then he plants some seeds around.
Shovels, rakes, and even hoes,
Help the farmer as he sows.

TRACTOR SONG

The wheels on the tractor go round and round,
Round and round, round and round.
The wheels on the tractor go round and round,
All around the farm.
The tractor in the field goes back and forth,
Back and forth, back and forth.
The tractor in the field goes back and forth,
All around the farm.
The farmer on the tractor goes up and down,
Up and down, up and down.
The farmer on the tractor goes up and down,
All around the farm.
(make up more verses: horn goes beep, engine goes chug)

FARM CHORES

This is the way we pull the weeds, pull the weeds,
Pull the weeds.
This is the way we pull the ways,
So early in the morning.
(make up more verses: drive the tractor, mow the hay)

WAY UP HIGH IN THE APPLE TREE

Way up high in the apple tree,
Two little apples smiled at me.
I shook that tree as hard as I could.
Down fell the apples.
Mmmmmm! They were good!!

APPLES

Red and juicy, shiny, sweet,
Apple you're so good to eat.
Crisp and crunchy, healthy, too,
This core is all that's left of you!

APPLES AND BANANAS

I like to eat eat eat apples and bananas,
I like to ate ate ate apples and bananas,
I like to eat eat eat apples and bananas,
I like to ite ite ite apples and bananas,
I like to ote ote ote apples and bananas,
I like to ute ute ute apples and bananas,
I like to eat eat eat apples and bananas.

APPLES HERE

Apples here, apples there,
Apples are everywhere.
Some are red, some are yellow.
Please give one to this hungry fellow.

APPLES

Pick some apples off the tree,
Off the tree, off the tree.
Pick some apples off the tree,
Some for you and some for me.

RED APPLE

A little red apple hanging on a tree.
The juiciest apple you ever did see.
The wind came past and gave an angry frown.
And that little apple came tumbling down.

MR. CARROT

Nice Mr. Carrot makes curly hair.
His head grows under the ground,
And his feet are in the air.
Early in the morning I find him in his bed.
I give his feet a great big pull, and out comes his head!

MY GARDEN

This is my garden.
I'll rake it with care.
And then some flower seeds,
I'll plant in there.
The sun will shine and the rain will fall.
And my garden will blossom, and grow straight and tall.

DIG A LITTLE HOLE

Dig a little hole, plant a little seed.
Pour a little water, pull a little weed.
Give a little sunshine, grow a little bean.
It grows big, and gets green and greener.

TOMATO

I'm a tomato, red and round,
Red and round, red and round.
I'm a tomato red and round.
I just fell on the ground.

CORNSTALK

I'm a cornstalk tall and straight,
Tall and straight, tall and straight.
I'm a cornstalk tall and straight,
And my corn tastes just great!

PICK UP THE SQUASH

Pick up the squash and put it in the basket.
Pick up the squash and put it in the basket.
Pick up the squash and put it in the basket.
Pick up all the squash.
(sing again using a different vegetable: corn, pepper, onion, potato)

ONE POTATO, TWO POTATO

One potato, two potato,
Three potato, Four.
Five potato, six potato,
Seven potato, more.

THIS IS MY APPLE

(sung to "You Are My Sunshine")
This is my apple, my shiny apple.
It makes me happy every day.
When I eat one, it makes me healthy.
Please don't take my apples away.

FARMER SAM

Farmer Sam, Farmer Sam,
Raises cows and hogs,
Chicken, sheep and goats and ducks,
And even friendly dogs.
Farmer Sam, Farmer Sam,
Also raises crops.
He plants the seeds and pulls the weeds
Until his crops are tops.

COLORFUL CROWS

Scarecrow (child's name),
Standing all alone,
Shoo that (color) crow back to its home.
(have laminated crows of different colors on the floor, when it is a child's turn he gets the crow of the color named and shoos it away)

BOBBY JOE THE SCARECROW

Bobby Joe is filled with hay,
Way down on the farm.
Oh, will he scare the crows away?
Way down on the farm.
Oh, the crows are here
And they want to stay.
Bobby Joe, Bobby Joe,
Can you make them fly away?
Bobby scared the crows away,
Way down on the farm.

I'M A LITTLE PUMPKIN

(sung to "I'm a Little Teapot)
I'm a little pumpkin, orange and round.
Here is my stem, and there is the ground.
When I get all cut up, don't you shout,
Just open me up and scoop me out.

HERE'S A PUMPKIN

Here is a pumpkin who is happy.
Here is a pumpkin who cries.
Here is a pumpkin that's sleepy,
Here is a pumpkin that sighs.
Here is a pumpkin that's angry.
Here is a pumpkin that's sad.
Here is a pumpkin that's noisy.
Here is a pumpkin that's glad.

J-A-C-K-O

There was a pumpkin with a face and JACKO was his name-0.
J-A-C-K-O, J-A-C-K-O, J-A-C-K-O,
And JACKO was his name-O!

FARM CROP UNIT

ACTIVITIES LISTED BY DOMAINS

SCIENCE ACTIVITIES

- Introduce scales for weighing plastic (or real) fruit/vegetables.
- Introduce a different vegetable or fruit every day—have it sliced so the children can use all of their senses to investigate.
- Have seeds for children to sort.
- Plant seeds and discuss what they need to grow.
- Chart the growth of plants in the room.
- If possible, prepare and care for a small outdoor garden.
- Cut the top off a real pumpkin, let children scoop out the seeds.
- Cook pumpkin seeds and eat.
- Make "stone" soup with the children.
- Let children taste a raw vegetable and the same vegetable cooked: graph which one they liked best.
- Sort healthy food from junk food.
- Conduct a grease test: have 2 folded paper towels, put grapes on one, put potato chips on one, gently press the folded part of the paper towel on the food, remove the food and see which paper towel has a grease spot.
- Discuss where foods grow: under the ground, on vines, or on trees.
- Discuss what plants need to grow: dirt, water, sunshine.
- Husk corn, cook, eat. (Have a corn husking race.)

- Boil potatoes, let children use potato mashers to make mashed potatoes.
- Use small milk cartons (cut off tops to make a small box), draw a face on the outside of the carton, fill will soil and grass seed, (water and place in a sunny area), the grass will grow and look like hair.
- Collect flowers and weeds, (press between paper and something heavy for 5 days), remove and seal between two sheets of contact paper.
- Grow seeds: put a lima bean on a moist paper towel, place the towel in a ziploc bag, tape bags to a window and watch the seeds sprout.
- Root a carrot: place a carrot root end down in a jar of water (cover 1/3 of the root) and watch it root (use toothpicks to hold the top of the carrot out of the water).
- Place celery stalks with leaves into a clear container, add 3 inches of water and some food coloring. In a few hours check to see what has happened to the color of the leaves. To make this experiment more interesting, split a celery stalk in ½ just up to the leaves (do not separate entirely), put ½ stalk in a container with one color of water and the other ½ in a container with a different color of water. Watch what happens to the color of the leaves.
- Put whipping cream into baby food jars, let the children shake the jars until a ball of butter forms, spread the butter on bread or crackers, eat.
- Conduct "taste tests": fresh fruit vs. dried fruit.
- Make cornmeal play-dough.
- Make applesauce.

MATH ACTIVITIES

- Weigh vegetables such as pumpkins and potatoes.
- Measure circumference of pumpkins.
- Measure height of cornstalks.
- Estimate how many apples will fit into a basket.
- Count apples and pumpkins.
- Look at the star shape inside an apple.
- Sort fruits and vegetables by shapes/colors.
- Sequence pumpkins by size—small, medium, big.
- Make a scarecrow puzzle.

- Have tomato vines with numbers under them, the child puts that amount of tomatoes on that vine. (use red circle stickers)
- Introduce coins and their value—put prices on plastic fruit and vegetables, let the children buy them by counting out the right change.
- Read the numbers of UPC codes on cans and boxes of food.

LITERACY ACTIVITIES

- Cut letters out of magazines, glue onto paper to spell their names (and names of peers).
- Spell names and words using ABC pasta, cereal, cookies.
- Have children repeat the ABC letter names and sounds.
- Sequence 3-4 story events.
- Children retell stories using props.
- Children generate and complete rhymes.
- Children use picture cards to match, compare opposites.
- Children keep a unit related journal.
- Children practice writing their names and ABCs.

ART ACTIVITIES

- Draw an apple on a white paper; children tear red tissue paper into small pieces, scrunch it, and glue it onto the white apple (make other tissue paper fruits and vegetables: green pears, orange pumpkins, etc.).
- Cut a potato in half, dip the potato into paint and stamp.
- Paint paper eggs cartons various colors, hang them from ceiling for an abstract art display.
- Make fruits and vegetables using stuffed lunch bags, paint, and cut out green leaves, and add green yarn for vines.
- Children paint bubble wrap, when dry it can be cut into corncob shapes to look like Indian corn.
- Children can use a corncob as a paint roller to make a unique design.
- Children can use popcorn in creating a picture.
- Make crop collages: each child is given a sheet of construction paper and told to draw a farm picture, they are then given rice, wheat, popcorn, seeds, etc. to glue on the picture to make a collage.

- Fingerpaint large cut-outs of fruits and vegetables.
- Use celery leaves as a painting tool.
- Paint with straw.
- Make a shoebox garden: make carrots (including the green leaves) using oak tag and construction paper; color the top of a shoebox brown, put glue on the brown lid and sprinkle sand on, make slits in the lid; stick the roots of the carrots into the slits until only the green leaves are showing; the children can practice pulling the carrots out of the garden.
- Paint with garden tools.
- Cut pictures of food out of the paper or magazines. Children glue their paper meals onto paper plates.
- Make corn cobs: cover toilet paper tubes with yellow cotton balls.
- Children pick fruits/vegetables out of a bag; graph how many they have of each.
- Children help make a real scarecrow: stuff real clothes with paper or straw, add a paper bag head and hat, make a face on the head, assemble.
- Lace cut out apples.

PHYSICAL DEVELOPMENT ACTIVITIES

- Play the *Wheelbarrow Game*: a child holds a partner's feet as they walk with their hands like a wheelbarrow. Beanbags can be placed on the wheelbarrow's back to a specific destination.
- Pull wagons outside.
- Pedal a toy tractor outside.
- Play the *Upset The Fruit Basket Game* : divide the class into two lines facing each other about 10 feet apart; the children in both lines are designated a "fruit name". The teacher says "*bananas switch*", the bananas switch from one line to the other. If the teacher says "*apples and oranges*" then children with those names switch from one line to the other. If the teacher says "*Upset the fruit basket*" all of the children move from one line to the other.
- Play the *Pass The Corn Game*: pass a corncob around the circle as fast as they can, if someone drops the corn they are out of the game. Make the game more challenging if they can not use their hands to pass the corn.
- Play with balloons, keep them from hitting the ground.

- Play vegetable toss: toss plastic vegetables (or bean bags) into farm baskets from varying distances.
- Rake and hoe in an outside garden.
- Do the *Chicken Dance.*
- Have an egg hunt outside. (the children can climb or slide to find the eggs)
- Lace vegetables and fruits.
- Discuss healthy and not healthy foods/ look at food pyramid.
- Create healthy menus.
- Make healthy snacks.
- Discuss hygiene for cooking.
- Discuss hygiene in preparation for eating a meal.
- Play country and square dance music for movement activities.
- Play musical chairs (instead of chairs uses boxes for "hay bales").
- Perform exercise routines.
- Learn children's YOGA.

FARM CROPS UNIT

CENTER IDEAS

DRAMATIC PLAY AREA

- **Garden Prop Box:** Add gloves, flower pots, watering can, trowels, straw hats, plastic flowers, vegetables, bird feeders, and wind chimes.
- **Farmer Prop Box:** Add denim overalls, bucket, stool, toy hoes and rakes, straw hat, flannel shirt, bandana, work boots, gloves, large box painted for a barn, basket, plastic vegetables, and a scarecrow.
- **Kitchen Prop Box:** Add pots, pans, dishes, utensils, furniture, aprons, oven mitts, plastic foods, tablecloth, napkins, and baskets.
- **Farm Stand Prop Box:** Add wooden crates of plastic foods, cash register, play money, baskets, bags, receipt book, toy scales, gloves, straw hat, and aprons.
- **Restaurant Prop Box:** Add tables, chairs, menus, dishes, foods, aprons, tablets for taking orders, trays, napkins, cash register, play money, toy credit cards, receipt books, bill holders, vases for tables, and chef hats.

LIBRARY AREA

- Add books on farming and farm crops.
- Add gardening books.
- Add picture and ABC books that include foods.
- Add books that discuss "good manners".

DISCOVERY/SCIENCE AREA

- Use a sand table: plastic vegetables, gardening tools.
- Use scales to weigh plastic/wooden foods.

BLOCKS AREA

- Add a toy barn.
- Add toy tractors and other farm vehicles.
- Add cylinders to stack (like cans in the market).

ART AREA

- Lace cheerios to make a cereal necklace.
- Use stamps of vegetables, fruits, and farm items.
- Use real vegetables to use as stamps or rollers to make designs.
- Use seeds, wheat, rice, pasta to make mosaics.
- Make pictures using ABC cereal, pasta.
- Paint with straw and celery leaves.

WRITING AREA

- Trace word cards of farm crops and farm tools.
- Make a book of their favorite foods—draw picture and write names.
- Write a grocery shopping list.

TABLE GAMES AREA

- Play with farm puzzles. (table and floor)
- Play with store bought toys such as Animal Planet Farm Bucket.
- Play with store bought Imagination Desk Talk and Sing Color Book: Tad's Counting Day at the Farm
- Have picture cards of farm tools and crops to use for memory/concentration games.
- Play Food Bingo Game.

- Play with wooden foods cut into different number of pieces; Velcro enables putting together to make a whole: introduction to fractions.
- Play with Mr. Potato Head.
- Play with cash register and toy money.

HOPE YOU AND YOUR CHILDREN ENJOY THE UNIT!!!

My apologies for unknown or uncredited sources. I have compiled these ideas, plans, and activities throughout my many years in the classroom.

Not for resale, redistribution, or multi-site use.

I can be contacted at:
carouselcurriculum@yahoo.com

Made in the USA
Middletown, DE
10 August 2022